THE LITTLE BOOK OF
RIGHT THINKING

THE LITTLE BOOK OF RIGHT THINKING

ITS

APPLICATION TO INWARD ATTAINMENT

AND OUTWARD ACHIEVEMENT

by

HENRY THOMAS HAMBLIN

Introduction by Stephanie Sorréll

Science of Thought Press Ltd.
Bosham House, Bosham, Chichester,
West Sussex PO18 8PJ, England

Telephone/Fax: 01243 572109
E-mail: scienceofthought@mistral.co.uk

First published 1921
16 reprints
Revised edition 1999

© Copyright:
Science of Thought Press Ltd.

Published by:
Science of Thought Press Ltd.
Bosham House
Bosham
Chichester
West Sussex PO18 8PJ
Great Britain

A catalogue record for this book
is available from the British Library

ISBN 1-903074-00-2

Typeset by Michael Walsh at MusicPrint
Chichester, West Sussex
Printed and bound by RPM Reprographics
Chichester, West Sussex

CONTENTS

INTRODUCTION TO THE WORK

"You must have this reprinted again," Margaret, a lady in her early 70s urged me, thrusting the small battered book into my hand. "I say this is still the most important book Mr Hamblin wrote. It's what the work rests on!"

It was my first day, five years ago, working as editor for the well loved and much travelled bi-monthly journal *New Vision* (formerly *Science of Thought Review)*. It was hard to believe that some 900 editions of the magazine and countless reprints of the twenty odd books Henry Thomas Hamblin had written, had emerged from those old wooden buildings which had been the workplace for over 70 years. Margaret had worked at Bosham House for 30 years on and off. She had been there in the days when Mr Hamblin was in his 80s, dictating up to 200 letters a day to his three secretaries.

In my hand I hold one of the few remaining copies of *Right Thinking* which I have almost had to keep under lock and key to stop them 'disappearing'. I have lost count of the amount of readers who have written in asking if we have any spare copies we can loan because they have lent theirs out or it has simply fallen apart through too much use. The copy I hold is no bigger than the span of my hand, yet it is immensely precious. Precious enough to have enjoyed 15 reprints since its first in 1921.

Like all works of great insight and wisdom, its text is simple and accessible. It is a practical guide to attaining inner peace and well being that has helped thousands throughout the world. Henry Thomas Hamblin, the author, was remarkable in that he lived what he taught, his whole life was an expression of all he had to base his philosophy on. Before devoting his life to the spread of this teaching he was a highly successful businessman, founding the well known Theodore Hamblin opticians in

Wigmore Street in the West End of London. But success had not come easily to the optician. Born into a poor family, he had no other desire than to break out of the rut of poverty he was in. His fragile physical health, nervous temperament and sensitivity made him search deep within himself for answers. As a young man he was described as wayward, and eternally restless which by the nature of his human frailty endears him to our hearts.

Although Hamblin was inherently a seeker of Truth by nature, it was the death of his ten year old son that really caused him to reach bedrock and give birth to his vision. The material world that he had worked so hard in did not bring him the fulfilment or peace he was looking for.

It was without any regret that at 50, he gave up his secure job and income to live in the house he rented in the harbour village of Bosham in West Sussex. With a wife and three children to support he had the opportunity to put all he believed into practise.

He simply built a wooden shed in the garden which was to be an office and started to write three books; *Within You is the Power, The Power of Thought* and *The Message of a Flower*. Simultaneously, he began writing courses on the lines of positive and applied right thinking. Because the courses became immensely popular in a relatively short space of time, Hamblin developed *The Science of Thought Institute* as an umbrella for his work. But popular though his courses were, Hamblin felt something vital was missing – the spiritual element. And here it is important to add the firm demarcation Hamblin made between religion and spirituality. Emerging from a deeply religious background he had retaliated against the dogma that felt more like a straitjacket about him than a safety harness. Although he was a Christian and a true mystic, he believed that his teaching was at one with the teachings of Buddha, Confucius, Lao Tzu, St Theresa and William Law. His trust and love of God was based on the need for truth and spirituality rather than religion. He believed that too often religion divided people, while spirituality and Truth united people.

So just when money was pouring in for the courses from students all over the world, he scrapped all his work and made a bonfire of the courses. He admitted that giving up his only source of income was a crazy thing to do, but the sense of 'calling' within him outweighed any sense of worldly logic. After that he sat down to create what was to become the twenty seven lessons of the second batch of course material. As always when he took the manuscripts to the printer he had no way of knowing how he would pay the bill, but since this was a normal state of affairs for him, he never let it faze him because, always at the last possible moment, the money came in. In his heart he knew that if he was working in harmony with the divine Plan, the universe would come to meet him. In actuality, this was to form the bedrock of his whole life teaching.

It was around about this time and through the suggestion of his students, he set up a monthly magazine called the *Science of Thought Review* based on this applied right thinking. Since he hadn't as yet acquired any writers, he wrote the entire first issue himself, then made another leap of faith by having 10,000 copies printed. He sold 1,200 copies to his students and gave the rest away. In no time at all subscriptions poured in, and he had to build an extension onto the wooden hut to accommodate the growing number of staff he needed to employ.

For a man who had no real publishing or advertising experience, but only a willingness to work hard to realise his vision, he must have fulfilled a deep hunger in humanity for his work to carry him into the millennium.

His straight forward pragmatic approach which overlaid the spiritual teaching appealed to readers of all ages and backgrounds, from top university lecturers and successful business men to housewives and people from spiritual backgrounds as diverse as Hinduism, Buddhism and the Quakers.

Although it wasn't Hamblin's intention to alienate people by using the word 'science' in the title, he did see this application of right thinking as a definite science with a measurable effect on the well being of the person who practised it, not least of all himself. It must be remembered that in the 1920s his work was revolutionary and an important building block of the New Thought teachings which were beginning to emerge at that time.

In the second *Science of Thought Review* magazine Hamblin drew up eight guidelines for members to follow:

1. Endeavour always to avoid negative thoughts of all kinds.

2. Think in harmony with the Good.

3. Live as pure and humane a life as possible.

4. Spend a few minutes once a day at least in the Silence (or meditating).

5. Obey the law of Love.

6. Help and bless others.

7. Spread the knowledge of right thinking.

8. Endeavour to further the truth of the brotherhood of man and God.

9. Become a subscriber to the magazine.

Although this is a revised edition of *Right Thinking*, other than replacing outdated words and modernising the text to fit modern day language, I have been reluctant to change some of the phrases that Hamblin used regularly in his work. Where meditation has miraculously found its way into the market place of every day life, I have retained 'The Secret Place of the Most High' to further enrich and distil the sanctity of the inner silence we seek through meditation, prayer and contemplation. This is not an attempt to put it out of reach, but rather to create a sense of presence in what we seek. Also I have retained the word 'student' for, as seekers of truth and inner development,we are eternally students as long as we are here engaging in this global school of learning.

Right thinking I believe is of paramount importance today where we live in an age where our minds are constantly bombarded with information. Since our lifestyles have become materially orientated it is even more essential to create a platform of right thinking upon which we can stand and remain centered. Without this platform we can easily find ourselves pulled in countless directions and at the end of the day, or week or even month find we are drained of will and purpose, our energy dissipated by the demands of modern day life. Just as it is no good visiting a petrol filling station unless we know how to work the pumps, we need to know how to train and harness our minds in order to access the spiritual nourishment that is within and around us waiting to be drawn from.

Mr Hamblin's motto was: "If you change your thoughts, you change your life". It is a simple or as difficult as we make it. But nevertheless this essential work is an ideal model or blueprint to work from to-day.

Stephanie Sorréll (Editor)

FOREWORD

Right thinking in a broad, elementary and general sense, is thinking positive thoughts instead of negative ones. It means entertaining thoughts of success instead of failure, health instead of sickness, love instead of hate, cheerfulness instead of gloom, optimism instead of pessimism, opulence instead of poverty, victory instead of defeat, liberty instead of bondage, and so on. One who does this becomes inwardly changed. Through being changed inwardly, one's actions also become altered, this, in turn, transforms our life and circumstances. Therefore, through the change from wrong to right thinking, the character or self becomes altered, hence the scripture fulfils itself: "Be ye transformed by the renewing of your mind."

Right thinking, however, in its highest sense, is something even greater than all this. It is thinking in an altogether higher consciousness and from an entirely new (to the individual) standpoint. It means thinking from the perspective of the universal Mind instead of the weak, limited, finite mind. It means thinking in the *actual consciousness* of love as the reality, perfection as the *reality*, health as the *reality*, harmony as the *reality*. It means liberation in thought from being enslaved by the senses and the desires. It means living the life in a higher octave, upon an altogether higher plane. In other words, it is possible to rise above the limitations of time and sense; to aspire to the consciousness of eternal life and being; to think *with* God instead of in the human finite way which is against Him.

Right thinking is also thinking and living in the consciousness that all is well. It is to know in *one's very soul*, that God's ways are perfect; that He makes no mistakes; that everything is working together towards the complete fulfilment of the divine Purpose. Right thinking also is to know that perfection exists as a reality *now*, and to think in the consciousness of this knowledge.

It must not be thought, however, that entering this higher consciousness turns us into some supreme being, because this is very far from being the case, but it does give us that revelation of truth which Jesus said should make us free. The difference between thinking with the finite limited mind and thinking with the universal mind is perfectly described in Isaiah, chapter 55: "For my thoughts are not your thoughts. Neither are your ways my ways, saith the Lord. For as the Heavens are higher than the earth, so are my ways higher than your ways, and my thoughts than your thoughts." Therefore, in order to think *with* God, which is the aim of every seeker after truth, it is necessary to rise high above the ordinary plane of human thought and to think in an altogether higher consciousness. Man, when he is ready for the change, is invited by God to make this change. In the same chapter we read: "Let the wrongdoer forsake his way, and the unrighteous man forsake his thoughts and let him return unto the Lord, and He will have mercy upon him; and to our God for He will abundantly pardon."

That it is possible to reach this cosmic or universal mind is abundantly proved both by human experience and in the New Testament. That Jesus the Christ could rise, at will, into this superconscious realm of the universal mind is perfectly evident. His teaching, for the most part, is given direct from the cosmic mind and standpoint, and is only understandable when this fact is recognised and understood. Undoubtedly he taught His disciples that it was possible also for them to rise into this higher mind of God.

It is from this higher plane or octave that all healing is done; it is from this superconscious realm that truth can be understood in such a way as to set us free.

Right thinking is the very reverse of impractical dreaming or mystical ecstasy. It is intensely practical. I can say, as a practical business man* who started life without a penny, and who had a rough and tumble fight with the difficulties and realities of life for many years, that there is nothing so practically helpful as right thinking. Having had to make my own way in life from a very early age without the help of either monetary influence, or education, in addition to being handicapped by delicate health, nothing appeals to me that will not 'cut ice'. Before I can accept anything I must prove its practical, definite usefulness.

The good effects which follow this higher right thinking in harmony with God, are described in poetic and symbolic language by the inspired prophet, Isaiah, who himself is speaking from the standpoint of the universal Mind. Isaiah says: "For ye shall go out with joy, and be led forth with peace; the mountains and the hills shall break forth before you into singing, and all the trees of the field shall clap their hands. Instead of the thorn shall come up the fir tree, and instead of the brier shall come up the myrtle tree; and it shall be to the Lord for a name, for an everlasting sign that shall not be cut off."

All the above promises have been proved, in practical experience, to be perfectly true. Those who learn this art and science of right thinking find, in course of time, that the thorns and briers of failure, fear, discord, hate, sickness, unhappiness and needless suffering, give place to true success, achievement, harmony, love, happiness and health. The prophet's words, when reduced to plain, ordinary language, clearly indicate that for those who think and act in harmony with God, instead of against Him, shall, here and now, in this life, enjoy harmony, peace, health, happiness and joy.

And it is far more than this, as the following pages will show. It brings with it a new conception of life. It says in effect that life is spiritual, that you cannot separate matter and spirit. It was Thomas Carlyle who said that matter could only exist spiritually, therefore man must exist spiritually or not at all. In fact, man is a spirit, and the physical body is merely his material and outward expression. If life is spiritual then man can be truly successful through spiritual forces; he can be healthy through spiritual forces; he can achieve and accomplish through spiritual forces; he can be happy through spiritual forces; he can love through spiritual forces. Therefore, the true art of living is the development, training and use of spiritual powers. There is no method of education that does this; it can never be achieved by objective means; it can be accomplished only by subjective processes. By 'spiritualised' right thinking it is possible to arouse and train man's inward powers so that he can achieve success in life, bring harmony into his home, health to his body, and by his joy and optimism bring brightness and happiness to all his companions. And more – it will enable him to unfold, to find within him the spark of divinity which for so long has been hidden.

This science and art of right thinking is also practical. It has taken a great truth and, brushing aside all that is not essential, has woven it into a practical system which can be applied with precision to all the problems of life. It has discovered that life is a result, an effect, and that the reality and cause are *within*. It teaches that life responds to certain laws, and that by working in harmony with these laws results can be obtained with mathematical precision. It disperses the vagueness, mystery and uncertainty which surround so many teachings, and shows how life can be governed by scientific methods. It teaches that the running of the universe is not whimsical but governed by immutable laws. "As a man soweth that shall he also reap" and "As a man thinketh in his heart so is he", are proved to be scientifically true. Just as man can harness the lightning, drive his trains and machinery by electricity, and light his streets and houses, so can man, when he understands the laws which govern his life, produce results none the less remarkable, and which can be predicted with equal certainty, because they are the effects of certain causes. We no longer need to feel fated or victimised by circumstances as we try to walk the mysterious path of life in darkness and uncertainty, relying upon chance or upon knowledge and understanding. Instead, we can govern our life with precision and certainty, and in this knowledge there is inner peace.

The importance of right thinking lies in the fact that all that we are ourselves, together with what comes into our life, are largely the result of our thoughts. It has been said that "we are what we think we are". It was Buddha who said: "All that we are is the result of what we have thought; it is founded on our thoughts; it is made up of our thoughts." The ancient Upanishad says: "What a man thinks, that he becomes." James Allen wrote: "Your own thoughts, desires and inspirations comprise your world, and, to you, all that there is in the universe of beauty and joy and bliss, or of ugliness and sorrow and pain, is contained within yourself. By your own thoughts you make or mar your life, your world, your Universe."

If our life is unhappy and 'out of sync' today, it is largely due to our wrong and disharmonious thinking in the past, the fruits of which we have to bear now. Every disharmonious thought brings, with mathematical exactness, its corresponding result. We cannot escape the effects of our thoughts for they come to us with perfect precision. "Whatsoever a man soweth that shall he also reap" is written in letters of gold on the portals of eternity, and it is so because the universe is not run by chance, but by exact and never failing nor varying law. Therefore, if our life is disharmonious, it is simply the effect of our thoughts, for everyone gets exactly the experience he needs. He who indulges in self-pity is wasting his energy, for whatever comes into his life is the exact result of his thoughts.

But you exclaim: "What about actions? What about sin?" My reply is that actions and sin are simply the result of wrong thinking. If we think evil, we express evil. If we allow wrong thoughts to enter our mind, they birth bitter fruits in due season. Wrong thinking is thinking out of harmony with eternal Truth and is responsible for much ill-health, restriction and unhappiness, as well as wrong actions of many kinds.

Some may say: "Well, if we cannot escape the effect of our thought, we may as well give up trying, and then where does your philosophy of joy come in?" The answer is that one's thoughts, as the result of self-training and self-discipline, can be controlled. Some people may say that it cannot be done; that thought is so elusive it cannot be controlled. Others will say: "I cannot control my thoughts; if I could I would cease to worry. As it is, as soon as the slightest trouble appears, I start worrying and fearing, and although I know that I am not doing any good by this, but rather harm, I cannot help myself," or "I am of a worrying nature." But that does not prove that thought cannot be controlled. It only proves that the speakers have not understood the art of scientific thought control. Thought can be controlled as a result of perseverance, patience and persistence. Great changes such as this cannot be accomplished in a day, but they can be achieved in course of time by systematic practice of right principles.

Granted then that it is possible to control your thoughts, let us consider the results which will accrue if right thinking is practised.

First, instead of destructive thinking there will be constructive thinking. Instead of struggling against life and creating difficult future conditions, the life and character will be built up in beauty and harmony. Instead of creating disharmony, a hostile environment, failure, and disease there will be a tendency to change these things into success, health, happiness, peace and joy.

Second, the powerful vibrations of constructive thinking, i.e., thinking in harmony with the infinite and universal Mind, will gradually change the character and transform the life. Harmony will be restored through thinking in line with eternal truth. The infinitely good life-force, which is the life of God, immanent in man will be allowed to manifest itself in consciousness in the form of good, such as health, harmony, achievement through service, efficiency, and sufficiency.

Life is not robbed of its discipline, but of its disharmonies and unnecessary suffering. Right thinking, that is, thinking from the perspective of truth, restores harmony, which is the normal condition. Good is positive, not a negative condition. Unfortunately, most people's idea of 'good' is entirely negative. To them 'good' is merely an absence of anything unpleasant. For instance, their idea of health is absence of disease; and happiness, to them, is mere absence of unhappiness. They know nothing of the abounding joy of health or the bubbling joy of the new life. God's life is perfect and, if allowed to flow unimpeded, can only manifest in the form of good. It is wrong thinking, false beliefs and absence of truth, that divert the good stream of God's perfect life into disharmonious channels, producing disease, poverty and other negative conditions.

Many people needlessly fear the effects of past wrong thinking and wrong actions. They say: "This is my karma, I must live it out." They become so saturated with this idea they aggravate and increase their troubles. Yet, if they would but believe the truth and realise and think and live in the consciousness of truth, they would find their troubles greatly lessened, if not altogether removed. It is useless to fight against life, but by meeting each difficulty with truth, and by thinking from the standpoint of truth, and living in the consciousness of truth, the life becomes transformed, and all its difficulties turn out to be friends in disguise. Additionally, as the character becomes changed, exterior influences and vibrations affect one less and less. Their power to hurt decreases as we rise to higher vibrations.

Detailed more fully in 'The Story of my life' by Henry Thomas Hamblin.

One

THE EFFECT OF THOUGHT

The immediate effect of thought upon our body, spirit, work, happiness, in fact every department of life, is so obvious that it seems hardly necessary to touch upon it. But experience with my students in the past has convinced me that some people are not awake to the power that thought exerts over their actions, and consequently over all that is the result of their actions. Therefore it may not be out of place if I touch lightly upon this subject.

A thought, someone has said, is an action in the process of being born. Everything that we do is the result of thoughts entertained or held in the mind. We may do things on the impulse of the moment, but that impulse is the result of a thought or thoughts previously held in the mind.

The subconscious mind is a centre of extraordinary energy and power. It is a blind force and acts upon suggestion. In other words, it acts upon the impressions which it receives from the objective mind and it depends upon whether these impressions, thoughts or suggestions are good or bad as to what sort of action the subconscious mind is going to bring forth in the life. The will and the moral sense must commence their defensive work with the thoughts and not with actions, because the former are the cause of the latter.

If therefore, one holds thoughts of a selfish character in the mind, then selfish actions will manifest in the life; if thoughts of pessimism then failure will be expressed; if thoughts of sickness and disease, then they will manifest in real sickness and disease in the body. If say, a young person says: "I don't think I can do a certain task", he will fail, but if instead he assures himself that be can do it, then his subconscious mind will do all it possibly can to help him to succeed, and unless he attempts something far beyond his stage of development, he will accomplish it. Good thoughts will produce good actions, and bad thoughts bad actions, and it is by controlling the thoughts that self mastery is to be found. All bad habits in the life and body have their origin in bad habits of thought, and good habits can be built up only by constructive, positive thinking, accompanied by corresponding right action.

If you say on a wet morning: "Isn't it a horrible morning!", then you make it a horrible morning for yourself and also help to make it unpleasant for other people, because you are not only sending an oppressive suggestion to your own subconscious mind, but you are doing the same to those who hear you. On the other hand, if you will take up the attitude that the weather might be a lot worse, that the rain is needed in the country, that the sun is shining gloriously behind the clouds and that everything is perfect in God's perfect world, you will transform the day into one of pleasure. Your own inner radiance and sense of joy cannot help but uplift those around you.

In the same way if you say to yourself: "I feel very bad today", then the subconscious mind acts accordingly. The message goes out to the millions of industrious little workers whose duty is the repairing, building up and keeping the body healthy, and they act accordingly. The whole system becomes depressed, the vitality is lowered, the powers of resistance weakened, so that you become easy prey to the first infection that you encounter. On the other hand, if when you feel off colour, you breathe deeply and as you breathe in affirm: "The Infinite is my health", and hold in the mind a thought or picture of perfect health, you will find that your condition will improve. The message of perfect health will be sent telepathically all over the body, and all the tiny fighters and workers will be inspired and encouraged to work on your behalf.

Again, in the same way, one who says:
"I am sure competition will ruin my business", is suggesting to himself his own failure. All his actions will unconsciously be
directed to this end, and time will inevita-
bly see the extinction of his business. Yet a
person in similar circumstances who states:
"No competition will be able to affect my
business. I will make my goods or my services so good that all my customers will, for
their own sakes, continue to deal with me",
because he is inspired by his own suggestion, he will work to make his services so
indispensable to the public that his business
will succeed more than ever.

By this, we can see how thoughts affect
our lives, and how it is only by controlling
the thoughts that the actions can be governed, and through the actions the very life
and environment itself.

Right thinking goes far more deeply
into this great subject than this. It teaches
that thoughts held in the mind attract, by

the law of vibration, the material for their objective expression. That actually what is held in the mind, with fine clarity of thought and inward vision, becomes manifested in the life; that each type of thought brings forth fruit of its very nature. It teaches that if there is confusion of thought in the mind, there is experienced confusion and disharmony in the life and circumstances, and that according to the thought and mental vision the life is either broken or blessed.

The practice of right thinking, additionally trains the mind to think only those thoughts which will harmonise with the immutable laws which govern the universe, bringing into the life the highest good, truest joy, the only satisfying success.

*For greater depth, readers are recommended to read **The Power of Thought** by the same author, listed at the back of this book.*

Two

THE GREATEST ACHIEVEMENT

The greatest message that this book brings to you is this: That man by working daily for a short time in the inner and higher mental and spiritual realm, can subtract the evil from his life and add good in its place. That is to say, by meditating upon the divine Perfection he becomes changed into its likeness. This will also destroy that influence in his life which he calls bad luck and ill-fortune, and replace it by certain and harmonious good. It will banish unhappiness and fill him with a great joy which has its source within and is not dependent upon outside circumstances. He can protect himself and others from danger, difficulty and disaster. He works with precision; he is not dealing with uncertain theories, but with immutable law which can never fail or alter. This is real prayer.

He does not do this by will power; he does it by harmonising with the Infinite. Real success in life is only to be found along this line of harmony with the Divine. Man is a spiritual being, and when he realises his own spiritual nature and learns how to draw upon the infinite powers within him by working in unity with his divine Source, his life becomes changed. Day by day a little negativity is taken out of his life, and day by day a little good is put in its place. Results are not seen at first, but they are cumulative, and in time are bound to manifest just as surely as the rising and setting of the sun.

Many people say: "What is this negative influence that follows me? As soon as I get on a little in business I suffer a severe loss. When I make plans for a happy life, disaster overtakes me and shatters all my hopes." There is nothing bad or negative following him; instead, what he is suffering from is absence of good due to the disharmony of his thought and life. When once the disharmony gives place to unity, then the transformation of the life begins.

But while any true system of thought control is training the student in these major things, it is also accomplishing minor changes, which make for success and stability in life. Will power, concentration, determination, perseverance, creative imagination, directed thinking, natural memory, the appreciation of beauty, self-confidence, cheerfulness and optimism, are all developed without the student being aware of it. I mention these things because they are of real value to the student, but they fade into insignificance beside the major objects which the practice of truth achieves.

Right thinking brings accuracy and precision into the life. It makes life certain and secure. It brings everything down to a system, a system which, if followed, gives mathematically certain results. By that I do not mean that it is wise to always decide for yourself what form 'good' shall take in your life; for it is very often better to leave this to the divine Mind. But the certainty and exactitude is in this, that by working steadily, persistently, and daily through the avenue of controlled, directed thought, towards the Source of all, from which everything proceeds, one is able to transmute negative life experience into positive energy. At first the old troubles and evils persist; with some they even get a little worse, but after a time it is noticed that the attacks are less severe, the trouble less acute, and from then onwards a steady and gradual improvement takes place, until the whole life and circumstances are transformed.

Three

HAPPINESS

Happiness is an inward mental state. It cannot be found in outward things. The idea popular with the masses that happiness is to be found in material possessions, in wealth, the means of gratification and luxury, is not shared by those who possess these things. The supposed happiness which the unthinking imagine is to be obtained by wealth and all that wealth can buy, is merely the glittering baubles of life towards which men stretch out eager hands, but whichever eludes their grasp.

Henry Victor Morgan in an exalted moment once wrote:

> *Today on the heights I stand*
> *Above the sea of thought,*

And look o'er the changing drift
At the baubles for which men fought;
That slip through their clinging hands
And ever remain uncaught.

Unchained through the drift of years.
They float o'er the surface clear;
And for ever warm hands reach out
As the illusions of life draw near;
ill the weary hands sink deep
And the eager new appear.

Happiness, then, is not to be secured by chasing the illusions of life, but by looking within where the only true reality lies.

Man is a spiritual being here and now, and his unhappiness is due to his lack of appreciation of this great fact. Man will always be unsatisfied until he realises he is a spiritual being, gifted with godlike powers; that he, as spirit, is one with the great Father of all spirits, the infinite Spirit, the Source of all things.

When he realises this astounding fact, the heavy load of care which has oppressed

him, the sense of his own loneliness and
friendlessness, the uncertainty and futility
of life, all disperse and he realises for the first
time the true inward meaning of happiness.

Happiness does not depend upon circumstances. The unenlightened say: "If only
my circumstances were better I should be
happy", yet if their circumstances were altered they would still be unhappy. Circumstances are not the cause of unhappiness, but
are the effect of the same cause; they are the
result of a lack of adjustment, and of an inward spiritual disharmony. The change
within which will cure our unhappiness will
cause the unhappy circumstances to disperse
also, for as soon as the lesson is learnt and
the necessary inward adjustment made, their
mission is finished. To long for painful experiences to pass away in order that one may
be happy is futile; the only way is to seek for
the cause of the trouble within, and make
the necessary adjustment to life and the universe. One who is unhappy is out of harmony with the eternal Will and the divine

scheme, and the unpleasant circumstances not only are the result of a wrong attitude of the soul, but they also seek to make one realise the cause, and to adjust the life accordingly. Happiness comes from within; it is the effect of harmonious adjustment with life; of coming into line with the divine Will and Purpose. Do not think for a moment that the divine Purpose is that our life should be boring, unhappy, painful or lacking in abundance and good. It may appear uninviting, but this is merely an illusion, for it leads to joy unspeakable, and happiness which cannot be described.

Again, there can be no happiness without service. To live a self centred, selfish life is the way of disintegration and death. It is the certain road to unhappiness, dissatisfaction and despair. Service to the whole, to life, to God, to humanity, to the universe, this is the way of harmony and inner satisfaction. No one who is self centred can be happy, for such a one is out of harmony with the divine Idea. Neither can he be at peace who carries out his daily work grudgingly. But one who works for the whole and makes his daily work a sweet offering of love to all life and humanity, enters the divine harmony; he knows what true happiness is.

Also, in order to be happy one must be able to exercise thought control. It is obvious that if happiness is an inward mental state, thought must have a lot to do with it. Those who cannot control their thoughts give way to fear and worry, or hate and anger, depression and gloom, and when this is the case happiness is impossible. One who does not make use of thought control is affected adversely by circumstances, by the disappointments and trials and testing times of life. But one who can control his thoughts is unaffected by these things. He can steer his thoughts away from dwelling upon everything negative and instead keep them fixed upon the one great positive reality of the universe – the infinite spirit of good and perfection. By doing this he loses all fear and unhappiness; he enters into infinite peace and joy. He leaves his weaknesses behind him, and filled with divine power, lives a life of tranquillity and victory.

Four

THERE IS A POWER

To the uninitiated, life is so material it is difficult to believe that behind the visible universe is a transcendental world of spirit which is the perfect reality of which the objective world is but an expression. Yet, this is true. The visible world, beautiful as it is, and marred though it may be by man's disharmony, is merely an effect or expression of the infinite reality. Metaphysicians who say that matter and the material universe do not exist, do so because, in a philosophical sense, only that which is permanent and unchanging can be said to exist. As far as this consciousness goes, however, the visible exists. If I have an abscess as large as my fist at the back of my neck, then, as far as this consciousness is concerned that abscess exists. It exists in my consciousness for a time and cannot be entirely ignored. On the one hand we have abstract thinkers who say that nothing material has any existence. Yet we also have concrete thinkers, materialists if you like, who cannot believe in anything that is not tangible. The truth is somewhere between the two. These are two halves to the complete whole. There is the unseen permanent reality, and there is the changing expression of that reality. There is the divine Idea, and there is the unfoldment of that perfection through endless change and evolution in material form. Matter is a vehicle of God's expression. It clothes His idea in form and colour. It is the outer garment of the spirit. To ignore either the material or the spiritual is to delude ourselves; they *together* form the One complete whole. In either case we ignore God, for God is the Creator of His universe; it is formed out of His spiritual substance; God's thought finds expression in His creation, therefore to deny matter and to call it evil is to deny God and call Him evil. Here, it might be appropriate to add that God is transcendent as well as immanent. In one sense, God is expressed in His universe, yet in another sense, He is not, for He is ever beyond it.

Matter then, and the material universe, are ever changing effects, ever evolving, ever unfolding more perfectly the divine Idea. The tremendous power that works through the universe is spiritual; it is the divine Mind in motion. This power is infinite; its object is to express on this material plane a perfect manifestation of the divine Idea. Its object is not to manifest disease, ill health, unhappiness, poverty, wrong doing, rather it is ever seeking to express itself in perfect health and harmony. The fact that there is unhappiness, sickness and poverty in the world only proves that man is out of harmony with his divine Source. Instead of divine life forces being allowed to flow freely and manifest good, they are diverted and made to produce negativity. The secret of all healing and true achievement is to remove the barriers which divert the spiritual forces of life, thus opening the life to the divine inflow.

This power is infinite; it flows in a constant stream from the unseen spiritual source into the material universe. We see it manifested in myriad forms, for God is immanent everywhere in His universe. We can look into the patient eyes of our animal friends and see Him there; we can gaze in rapture at the loveliness of a simple flower, or the grandeur of a crimson sunset and behold the beauty of His character. God is everywhere and in everything; to know this is to enter a new life of fullness and joy. We see the infinite Power manifested in all the wonders of the universe; in the evolution of worlds and system of worlds; in the immense power of nature; in the life which repeats itself through the ages.

In man, God enters into a new relationship with His creation. In man are the possibilities of a wider and deeper consciousness. Man stands at the apex of creation; he is the highest product of nature. All the kingdoms combine to produce him: mineral, vegetable and animal all minister to him and own him as Lord of creation. Man's feet are on the earth and his head in the heavens; He has within him, still lying latent, the possibilities of Godhood. He alone of all creation can think with God, commune with Him, enter into His consciousness, and become, in the course of time, one with the Infinite.

Man, being what he is, can draw upon this infinite power in a special way. He can, through the divine power of his mind and thought, consciously identify himself with the Infinite and draw unlimited power from his divine Source. There is no height to which he cannot climb if he will only keep his face to the 'light' and draw upon the inexhaustible fountains of God. "All power is given unto me in heaven and in earth," said Jesus, and of us, his weaker brothers, the same glorious fact is true. Man has thought himself to be a worm, but this is true only of his finite false personality; actually, he is called to be a king and priest unto God. Man thinks he is a creature of a moment; he gropes about in the ashes of his material life while above him is the glorious crown of his divine heritage. He languishes in weakness when he might instead be filled with infinite power.

The power is infinite, it is in you and in me; it is in all people. Very few know of this power, a still smaller number know how to *use* it. The majority would be very surprised, if not shocked were you to tell them that within them lie dormant infinite and divine powers, that within each of them is a spark of the divine fire, an inherent perfection which is patiently seeking expression. Yet, this is true; the power within us is infinite. It is divine. It can revolutionise you if you will but realise its presence, and allow it freedom of expression.

The power is the same as it was in the days of miracles; the law does not change. Those who adjust their lives in such a way as to bring them into harmony with the divine Law are healed. They express more and more of the infinite perfection, not just in their body, but also in their character. The power is the same, no matter how it is employed. It can be used to strengthen the body, give power to the mind, or bring the highest achievement into the life. No one who draws upon the infinite power and wisdom can ever be a failure; his life reflects the infinite achievement of God.

Five

TRUE PROSPERITY

The true prosperity is not the accumulation of great wealth. To be truly prosperous is to have the use of enough to enable one to live without struggling and yet to be free from the joyless burden of wealth. The truly wise is he who chooses to have enough and yet not too much, for while too little is irksome, to possess wealth is to assume burdens and responsibilities which are not worthwhile.

Some readers will raise the moral question of whether it is right to be even comfortably well off while so many are in need. This is, of course, a question for each individual to settle for himself. Personally, I think one is justified in accepting from life enough material things to enable one to develop and unfold on all planes, physical, mental and spiritual. One is therefore entitled to receive all that is necessary for one's highest development if one is prepared to give one's best services in exchange to mankind and the world. One who gives his best service, his best thoughts, his best emotions to life, the world and his fellows is entitled to an adequate return in the form of the best that life can give. But he who thinks he is 'clever' and by cunning tries to cheat life and his fellow man, taking much and giving little or nothing in return is not really clever, but only foolish, for what he gains in one direction he loses in another. He may gain money, true, but loses all the best and most satisfying qualities and gifts of life. Ones which money cannot buy. The way to true prosperity is through highest service, a changed dominant note of the inner mind, and understanding of truth through right thinking. This brings us into line with the divine law of giving and receiving; it also removes the mental cause of lack and poverty. This brings into the life a wise opulence, neither too much nor too little, and the sure knowledge that we can never lack any good thing.

One who does not understand the working of the divine Law is always afraid of poverty. He may be passing rich, yet, at the back of his mind is the haunting fear that he may lose it all and come into need. He so fears the future and what it may bring that he must hoard up money; something to fall back upon if things go wrong. Not satisfied with what he already has, he strives after greater riches in order to make himself 'safe'. This is the worship of Mammon. So long as we look to money and material means in themselves as our source of supply, so long as we think that these things keep us from want, we serve Mammon and therefore cannot serve God.

One who acknowledges that God (universal Mind and Spirit, if you prefer the term) is the Source of all supply, and daily and hourly realises his oneness with this infinite Source, can never lack any good thing. All that he need trouble about is to see that he gives his best and most efficient service to life in exchange for the abundance that he receives. One who cannot yet see God's bounty visible in his life should act, as far as service and thankfulness are concerned, as though it were *already* in manifestation. It is sure to come sooner or later, that is, if fear thoughts and limitation thoughts are transmuted into thoughts of God's plenty, as the reality, behind the lack and poverty of the unreality. This is the *true* prosperity—the *real* opulence.

It must not be thought, however, that one can sit still while the best things of life drop into one's lap. One must first be active mentally and spiritually in the inner world of thought, and then work physically. Life is mainly action; therefore to be worthy of prosperity one must work. Work, when well loved, is one of the greatest joys of life. No one can be happy or healthy who does not engage in plenty of work, not directed merely to his own selfish ends, but work given as an offering of love to life and the world.

It is not claimed that right thinking will suddenly convert a poor person into a rich one, neither does it dangle a get-rich-quick scheme before you. But it does train you to stop attracting poverty into your life, and instead put you on the road which, if pursued, will lead to a carefree sufficiency. It does show you how to stop the negative habit of thought and negative mental attitude which, by their vibration, keep success away. It also shows you how to enter into harmony with immutable law and, consequently, come under the law of attraction. It does show you how to do something with your mind which will take a little negativity and poverty out of your life and put a little good and prosperity back into it instead. This enacted several times a day will have a cumulative effect on the life which will in time begin to manifest itself and increase from year to year.

Some of my readers who are idealists may say that, if they accept more than a mere pittance for their work, they will have more

than their fair share and consequently rob
the poor. Yet, in reality, this is far from being the case. Our source of supply is *spiritual* and not material. God is not poverty-
stricken. He is infinite abundance itself. As
children of God, all the abundance of God
is ours, not for selfish use or enjoyment, but
for the use of and service to the whole. The
conditions of our lives are an outward expression of our thoughts and attitude of
mind. If our thoughts for ever centre round
a belief in lack and limitation, then these
things manifest in the outward life, for the
outward life reflects our thought life. Our
outward life is largely composed of our
thoughts clothed in material form. It is not
the reality. The reality is perfect. Your life
and mine are imaged in God's mind as perfect. By wrong thinking and false beliefs we
hide the truth from ourselves, thus mani-
festing imperfection instead of perfection.
Perfection, however, is still the only reality,
and all imperfection is caused by a materi-
alisation of our thoughts which hide the

truth from us. Our life has always been imaged in the divine Mind as perfect, even before the beginning of time, and all our needs are abundantly supplied and always will be, even when time itself shall cease to be. The object of our teaching is to bring those who are willing to that stage known as realisation. At this stage the truth is understood by the soul, the kingdom is found, after which "all these things shall be added unto you".

A practical application of the teaching of Jesus is the only way by which the problem of supply can be solved for all time, once and for all. When once we find the kingdom, we find that all our needs are supplied at just the right time, according to our faith and understanding.

If we look at nature around us we find no evidence of poverty in the divine Idea. Everywhere we see prodigal abundance and lavish profusion. Thousands of acorns to form a single oak; and enough energy devoted to flowers alone to clothe every son of man in material plenty. God is not poverty stricken, and those who enter into harmony with the divine Idea can never lack any good thing.

Some of us may feel that we are beaten in the selfish battle for material existence. The egocentric and ruthless may elbow us aside, trample on us, and make off with that which we would like for ourselves and our loved ones. We may feel that we are like sheep amongst wolves. This is very true; for spiritually-minded people are different from the worldly, and generally are on the losing end if they adopt the worldly methods. Even if they succeed they find that what they have won can be held only by strain, effort and force. Every man's hand is against them and they experience friction continually.

Now the true, spiritual way of working is to seek the prosperity that comes from the Infinite, or what the Old Testament would call the blessing of the Lord. When God, or the Spirit is blessing us, or when we are in harmony with spiritual law, prosperity comes to us without effort and strain. It comes gently like the falling of a soft rain. Unlike the prosperity of the materialists it does not bring unhappiness and disillusion, but rather, brings with it harmony and peace. God wants us to live happy, free, healthy and joyous lives, and if we obey His laws, He adds His blessing in the form of a prosperity that brings no care or sorrow, but only adds to our harmony and joy.

In order that there should be no misunderstanding, let me say that this is entirely different from the method of visualising what you want and compelling it to appear. This method, which involves the will, is a lower form of psychism and it is not a spiritual way of working. Although it may appear to be successful, it invokes the law of karma along with all that is involved.

Six

HEALTH AND HEALING

Health is the birthright of every human being. If we are sick, diseased, or suffering from prolonged ill health, it is because we are out of harmony with the divine plan. The vigorous health of our ancestors is gradually giving way to a more fragile health because man is becoming more sensitive mentally and spiritually. Therefore, he depends more and more upon mental and spiritual forces for his life and health. In actuality, we are becoming more nervous and highly-strung, more imaginative, more sensitive to the power of thought and other spiritual and psychic forces. This is why man must look more and more to the one Source of life for his health, energy and vitality.

Right thinking carries a message of health. It maintains that this mysterious thing which we call 'life' is a manifestation of God, and that it is only by going right back to the first cause, the Source of all Life, and adjusting our lives into harmony with spiritual laws, and by identifying ourselves consciously with this infinite power, that we can find true healing. Once this is done, disease and ill health pass away, not to reappear in another form, but leave the life for ever.

But it must not be thought that health is simply the absence of disease, for it is far more than this. To be well implies a certain flexibility of spirits, or possession of tremendous energy or at least a supply sufficient for all your needs. It means being fit and alive and full of joy both in work and play. One is in tune with the whole universe as well as one with the Source of all Life and infinite good.

To one who has gained perfect health by spiritual means, all things are indeed divine. Every blade of grass, every opening flower, the nodding trees, the whispering breeze, all speak to his soul and fill his heart with ecstasy and infinite content. Not only can man, through coming into harmony with the divine Source himself become healthy, he can also help others to attain better health. I do not say that everyone possesses all the qualities necessary to become a successful spiritual healer, but everyone who finds health himself can also teach others to do the same.

Seven

ABSOLUTE CERTAINTY

There is no chance or luck in the universe, all is unfailing law. The old idea of appeasing an angry deity is founded upon ignorance of this divine Law. Fortunately for us there is no condition or favour; all is according to immutable Law and absolute Justice. Divine spitefulness and divine favouritism do not exist, but eternal justice reigns supreme. We cannot curry divine favour; we must stand on our own feet, and as we sow, so shall we also reap.

Fortunately then for us, the universe is governed by universal Law and infinite Justice. This Law and principle never alter, never fail, and never cease to operate. We therefore have only to work in harmony with the divine Law to obtain absolute certain results. So long as man is ignorant of the Law and works against it, so will his life be filled with discord and what is called bad luck. There will be no certainty about it, for sometimes things will run smoothly, and he will say 'his luck is in'; then all at once troubles and disasters may come thick and fast, and he will say 'his luck is out'. But when man learns to know the Law and how to work in harmony with it, he begins to gain exact results. He may not be able to tell what exact form it will take, but he will know with absolute certainty that good will manifest in his life as a result of something which he has initiated in his thought world, and as a result of right decisions and right conduct. He may not know when it will be manifested, but he will know with certainty that it will be manifested. For example, someone may have suffered from a physical weakness or condition for twenty years or so and in spite of innumerable consultations with specialists and every kind of treatment both orthodox and complimentary have gained no relief, yet as soon as he brings his mind and life into harmony with the Divine, and works daily in accordance with certain laws, then he can rest assured his condition will slowly improve. Although the improvement may be infinitesimal it is cumulative and therefore ongoing.

It is the same with our circumstances and environment; we can bring ourselves into harmony with the Infinite and through working daily in the inner world improve our circumstances in the outer world. So long as we obey the Law and work constructively on the inner level, results will keep accumulating until at last they manifest in the outward life. The results must come; Divine Law always responds. The power never ceases to operate; *God can never fail.*

I do not care how negative a person is, nor how unsuccessful he may have been, nor how weakened by sickness and bad habits he is; if such a one will persevere and work according to this divine Law, and persist and keep on in spite of lack of visible results at first, he will surely succeed, *he can never fail.*

I know now, although I have not always known it that if I pray in the right way I can never really fail. Results *always* come with mathematical exactness; there is no human element in this Law; it is absolute; it is perfect; it is exact.

If I pray in the right way and act accordingly, only good can come to me. It may not always be according to my human idea; but will always be the very best for me, according to infinite Wisdom.

Eight

MASTERY OF FATE

Again on the heights I stand,
Where God's winds sing lullaby,
And no more I reach for the gleam
Of the baubles for which men die —
For I reach to the heart of God
And Master of Fate am I.

Henry Victor Morgan

What do we mean by fate? The simplest definition is that it is those events over which we have no control. The more we understand the power and effect of our thinking the less we find in our life that is out of our control. But still there are some things which appear to be quite unavoidable, for instance, our parents, date and place of birth, country of origin, death of relatives, and other big events in life. Then again, what man or woman is there who, having reached mid life, has not passed through an experience which defied all his or her powers of mind, body and soul, all his or her wealth or means, the help of friends and even frenzied prayers? Most of us are compelled to acknowledge that life is too big for us to handle and that there are events in it that are beyond our power to control.

There are those, however, who go much further than this. There are learned people who say that nothing happens; that we merely come up against things. They say that life is like a journey on a train, say from London to Edinburgh. The argument is that when we start on the journey, Edinburgh and all that lies between, are in existence, and that the reason we cannot see them until we reach them is simply due to limitations of sight etc. In the same way, it is argued that all the events of our life are already in existence, but we only experience them as we are swept along by life to come up against them, one by one. The fact that we cannot see the end from the beginning is due to limitations of consciousness.

Then there are those who are learned and skilled in esoteric and occult science. And although I am not skilled in these things, neither do I wish to be, I have been interested enough to try to find out how far the claims of these people could be substantiated. Although very sceptical I was forced to admit that up to a certain point their calculations and inferences were correct. Although I am still of the opinion that astrology and similar areas of the occult are better left alone, I have come to the conclusion that skilled astrologers can predict in a broad way what a man's life will be. In some cases their calculations may even prove to be very accurate. But this applies only so long as a man allows himself to be a creature of impulse, and a victim of circumstances.

Immediately a man begins to use his inward powers the astrologers fail; for he no longer follows his horoscope, but strikes out on a line of his own. Directly a man looks to God for help and raises his thoughts heavenwards he rises above the influences and impulses which otherwise would make him fall into serious error and trouble. When a man resists a temptation, in the strength of the Spirit through raising his thoughts to God he breaks the bonds which bind him; that is, he becomes free from that predetermined life which the horoscope forecasts. Every time that we control our thoughts, refusing to let them run in one direction and compelling them to flow into a higher more positive one, we break free from our bondage. In other words, *we master our fate.*

The life of the awakened man cannot be predicted. He becomes a liberated soul. He becomes freed from the law of sin and death. He strikes out on a new path of victory and overcoming.

Nine

SELF CONFIDENCE

Lack of self confidence is a cause of failure to many. They have the ability, they are ambitious, they have ideas, but they lack sufficient trust and belief in their own powers and ability to succeed, which is the priceless possession of all people of achievement.

All successful people are splendidly self confident, and no one who does not possess this spiritual quality – for it *is* a spiritual quality – can ever succeed. I have never met a successful person yet who did not utterly and absolutely believe in himself or herself. Neither have I ever met an unsuccessful person who was not lacking in this quality.

Right thinking develops self confidence in that it frees us from fear. What would some of us not give to free ourselves from fear and mistrust? Yet it can be done, and the process is not difficult. But far more important than this is the seeker learns to explore the wonders of his own interior mental and spiritual powers, and gradually trains them and uses them. When the seeker discovers he or she can draw upon limitless powers, and can call upon inexhaustible resources, there develops within the mind confidence, certainty and a perfect trust in these inward powers. The seeker instead of saying, "Can I do it?" says, "I can do it", and believing what he says goes and does it, relying upon the inward power to carry him through, and this power *never fails.*

The inherently successful man believes in himself and because of that succeeds. The trained student believes in the unlimited powers of the universal Mind which he can, by using his powers of thought, call upon and use whenever he needs. In addition, he knows and understands the Law, and is prevented from making mistakes in life which those with less knowledge are liable to fall into and, consequently, make a mess of their lives. Therefore knowledge of truth not only frees us from fear, making us more confident, it also imparts knowledge and wisdom by which the life can be guided into a lasting and abundant success.

When man realises his oneness with the Infinite he can never fear lack of self confidence. He knows that all the divine forces are his; they seek to obey his will and minister to him. Though his feet are still on the Earth, his mind is in God; his heart thrills with a sense of universal and unlimited power.

Ten

PEACE

The right thinking philosophy is practical, and one of its most helpful teachings is that there is a higher mental realm into which, after a little practice one can attain. Furthermore, it is accessible to all who will persevere. With practice one can retire into this higher realm and look down, as it were, with unconcern, upon the fever of life. In this upper strata of consciousness one is entirely released from all worry, disappointment, grief and fear, or whatever it is that seeks to mar the life and disturb the mind. From this height one sees all the ambitions, greed and selfishness of the material life in their true perspective. One sees things in the light of eternity, one sees from the universal standpoint and this cleanses the mind from every care and trouble, and enables one to enter into perfect peace.

Anyone unpractised in this area who, after reading these words, tries to enter this higher mental realm, will find it impossible. This is due to lack of thought-control and knowledge of how to use the mind. It is only through thought control and concentration that one can, dismiss all worrying thoughts and enter the realm of perfect peace and calm.

It must be pointed out, however, that in addition to thought-control, it is necessary to adjust the life into harmony with the laws which govern the universe. Students are shown how to free themselves of fear, and adopt an attitude of mind towards life which is in harmony with the purpose of the divine scheme. When the right mental attitude is attained the student enters into harmony with the whole object and purpose of life; he enters into union with God; he thinks with God; he enters into the divine consciousness; he continually lives in the peace of the Infinite.

Eleven

SELF DEVELOPMENT

The great object of this life is the development of character. This life is an opportunity given us to build up our character in certain directions. For instance, one person may have to overcome fear and worry, and develop trust. All the experiences of such a one's life will give him opportunities whereby he may fight this weakness. Another may have to overcome greed and selfishness, and he, too, will be given opportunities of fighting his failing, but whatever the weakness is, it must be overcome. If we allow our life to slip by without overcoming our weaknesses, then we are in a bad way, for we shall have missed the very purpose of life. All true 'thought' systems teach methods of overcoming weaknesses which, while not a royal road to quick and easy success are a great help on the path.

There is no quick route.

One who has not discovered his inner spiritual powers tries to conquer by will power alone. This is a joyless, painful and unprofitable method, and is extremely exhausting. The will should never be used in this way; instead, the inward spiritual power should be employed and directed by the divine Will. It is by this means alone that final victory can be achieved. All weaknesses and habits can be overcome by consciously using this inner power, but not without effort. It is a struggle between the higher self or lower self.

Self-control is possible only through thought control, for all action is the result of thought. One who cannot control his thoughts can never govern himself; he is literally a slave to his emotions and passions; he is a prey to every adverse condition which he meets. All habits can be mastered by using this technique. It is the same with every weakness of character; no matter what the weakness may be, it can be overcome by patient effort; by drawing upon the infinite power within; by thought-control, and through directed constructive harmonious thinking. Lying dormant within each one of us is a spark of the divine perfection. The greatest object of this life is bringing the Divine into manifestation. We can do this only as we build up character, overcome habit and learn self-mastery, but not without effort.

Twelve

INSPIRATION AND INTUITION

The ordinary mind of the senses learns from objective experiences, from the often misleading evidence of the senses, from books, from the experience of others. It possesses no inspiration, no originality, no genius. All inspiration comes from within. Within each of us are divine powers lying dormant and unexpressed. Inspiration is one of them, and one who makes a daily practice of entering the 'Secret Place of the Most High' experiences what is termed inspiration or direct knowing. One who receives inspiration in this way has received a call to service through inward inspiration. Emerson used to go into the woods and listen to the 'voice of the woods.' Great scientists and inventors have been 'struck' by insight but, all of these ideas come from within, not from outside.

Within us also are powers of intuition or direct knowing which can be unfolded and used for our own guidance and the blessing of others. It takes time and needs patience to unfold these powers, but when it is accomplished one is in touch with the deep wisdom of God.

Again, all originality comes from within. The surface mind can only copy the work of others and deduct by reasoning from known facts; true originality comes from the God within us. One who starts out on a fresh line of endeavour, or who brings a new idea to man, does so because he is divinely guided and instructed. We are each, if we could realise it, instruments through which the divine Mind brings light and guidance to men. By looking within to our divine centre we learn to think constructively and creatively, we enter into fellowship with God, we become creators with Him.

One who learns to use his inner mind is greatly helped in the journey of life; he can, by relegating a problem to his inner mind, find a solution to every difficulty.

We are told that Abraham Lincoln, truly a giant among men, when confronted by a perplexing problem, would dismiss it from his conscious mind and think of other things. After a time, when he came back to the subject, the answer was waiting for him, solved by his inner mind. Many business people when perplexed by a difficulty, to which there has apparently been no solution, withhold decision until they have 'slept upon it'. Unconsciously they are letting their inner mind solve their problem for them while they sleep.

One who lives a pure and good life and aspires after God, seeking only the noblest and best, will, if he uses his inner mind, be led to the highest good and will be taught how to express the divine within him in the most efficient service to his fellow man.

Thirteen

SUCCESS AND ACHIEVEMENT

Success can only be won through spiritual power. He who cannot succeed shows that he has not learned to use his inner spiritual and mental powers. William Pollard, a Quaker and historian, writing on the spiritual basis of civilisation, says:

"There is no opposition between the spiritual and the material... Far from there being any opposition, all material things good for man are discovered and made available by the use of his spiritual powers, and as long as he lives on this earth all his spiritual powers depend for their exercise on his body being supplied with air and food and drink ... Economic advantages are a real asset which count for much; but they count for much very largely because they tend to fall into the hands of the spiritually vigor-

ous races which have the energy and the ca-
pacity to make the best of them…There is
more need at this day than in all our history
for the secular spiritual gifts without which
civilisation cannot remain stable – for the
powers of leadership, organisation, foresight,
imagination, initiative, in all their degrees.
The gifts are here. God has bestowed them
abundantly on the human race… There is a
spiritual power which makes not only for
success, but for righteousness, and which
demands righteousness, as the condition on
which any lasting success is attained."

Success, then, depends upon spiritual
power, and true lasting success can only be
founded upon righteousness, justice, forgiveness and compassion to others. Every so-
called success which is founded upon power,
coercion, cruelty, exploitation and harshness
to others, has within it the seeds of its own
decay.

Fourteen

GOOD

To know and realise that through life and the universe runs the principle of infinite good is the first step towards happiness and success. To know that by consciously identifying oneself with the spirit of infinite good one can draw into one's life and body nothing but infinite good is to step out into a life of power and accomplishment.

God is infinite good; there is no evil in the divine scheme. When I look at a simple wayside flower, I realise in my soul that in beauty there is no evil; that there is only infinite good. Man possesses the divine power of thought. Thought is mind in motion; it is a spiritual power, and is greater than any material power. Through the misuse of this power man turns the good forces of life into wrong channels, and thus produces what we call evil.

War, addiction and cruelty towards others as well as self inflicted are all the effect of wrong thinking. The power of evil is the collective effect of wrong thinking. If people could have right thought and cultivate love, then war, together with other disharmonies would end. Our divine Elder Brother taught us to think harmoniously and in love, but sadly, men have ignored His teaching. As a result, we have witnessed the strange anomaly of so-called Christian nations fighting one another with every imaginable cruelty. The power of providential energy can be directed by our thoughts into either good or negative courses; therefore, if we, by right thinking, direct it into the right channels, it manifests through harmony, peace, happiness, health and joy.

By wrong thinking man turns the good forces of life into disease, sickness, poverty and every kind of disharmony. But by thinking with God instead of against Him, we can manifest health, abundance and highest achievement; we can enter into peace, we can live a life of overcoming and indescribable joy.

Fifteen

THE PATH OF ATTAINMENT

The path of attainment is the way along which the soul passes in its climb from lower to higher things. It is not an easy path, because it does not follow that because one treads this path and makes the steep ascent to God, that one's outer life should be either poor or lacking in achievement. Indeed, the outward life should reflect the progress of the greater life within. The one should compliment the other; for in the inner life we learn the secrets of God's power, the strength, the perfection of His character, and in our outer life we should express these in the form of true success and achievement. The things which we achieve in life are not in themselves important, but the effect upon our character through the mastering of difficulties is of lasting benefit. For instance, to build up a big business is of no value in itself, for it brings added care and responsibility, and the things which can be bought with money quickly pall and cease to satisfy. But while achievement of this kind has no value in itself, its character building effect is very valuable indeed. In the building up of a big business very high qualities are developed. One who builds up a huge business, and who keeps it, is tested and tried in every possible way. He has to exercise patience, courage, firmness, perseverance, faith, hope, self-control, vision and other qualities. The greater his difficulties, the more these qualities are developed. The business itself and the income that it brings are of little importance. Indeed, they are a great burden and responsibility and a comparatively poor man living a simpler life in a cottage is in all material respects better off; but the character building effects are priceless. These qualities, won through ceaseless strife and overcoming, are added to the soul permanently. They remain with the soul all through the ages. They become part of the real spiritual man.

It will be seen then that in the outer world of achievement we are given an opportunity to manifest god-like powers to develop qualities of character through achievement and overcoming. It is not the path of everyone to become the architects of great businesses, neither are we all called to be great lawyers, politicians, writers or artists, but it is possible for each one of us to achieve success in the particular work which we have come here to do. Whatever our work in life may be, we have the ability, lying dormant within us, to achieve success in that work. In the doing of our work, in overcoming its difficulties, we build up character and qualities of mind and soul which are eternal and enduring in quality.

Even if we cannot achieve what the world calls success, we can enjoy the satisfaction of doing our work better than ever it has been done before, or as well as it is possible for it to be done, or for us to do it.

But it must be added, life is not what it seems to be. It is not governed solely by the harsh ways of men. Instead, it is controlled by *spiritual* laws and forces. It does not matter how shut in we may appear to be, nor how hopeless our outlook as regards promotion, advancement, improvement in circumstances or environment may also appear to be, there is nothing that can keep us from rising and advancing, and there is no one who can interrupt our progress but ourselves. The reason for this is that life is spiritual and is governed by inner laws. The Law is that as soon as we are ready for promotion we get it, and when we have outgrown one position in life, another and more advanced and responsible position opens up before us. The story of a person's advancement and achievement is the history of his mental expansion. As soon as he has assimilated one set of experiences and outgrown one position, other experiences and a higher position open before him. Therefore, if our future seems hopeless, it is only because we think it is so. All that we have to do really is to expand our mind, to push back its boundaries, and to think in larger ways. The same law applies to all walks of life and all modes of activity. The individual must first grow and expand in himself, before he can grow and expand in life's achievements. This growth and expansion has its origin in the thoughts. We must train our mind to think big thoughts and then to follow this up with hard work and the discipline that all progress demands.

Sixteen

THE HARMONIOUS LIFE

The harmonious life is possible only to those who are harmonious thinkers. The outward life is a reflection of the greater life within. If our life is disharmonious it is because of disharmonies within and it can only become harmonious when we inwardly adjust ourselves to the motive of life and the purpose of the divine scheme. All the disharmonies of life, its discords and irritations, have their cause within us and not outside us. The mind of the senses would have us look outside ourselves for the cause, but the inner teaching tells us to look within. The average person lays the blame on life, fate, other people or God, and often becomes very bitter about it. The longer we look outside us for the cause, and the more we lay the blame upon others, the worse our troubles grow, and the more conflicting our life become. The cause of conflict is not in other people or in outward circumstances; it is not in fate, neither is it the vindictiveness of God.

It is, instead, lack of adjustment with the purpose of life; lack of unity with the cosmic whole; it is disharmony with divine Will and Purpose.

If we return to the divine Source and harmonise our inner life with its purpose running through the whole cosmic scheme, we live a life of harmony and peace. We literally live in God; think with God; work with God and become attuned to the divine harmony. Our life expresses peace and love and reflects the calm of the Infinite. The things which formerly frustrated our hearts no longer affect us. We live our life in a higher vibration. Full of love and sympathy, we help others and endeavour to lead them to higher things. By the harmony of our own life we become a restful influence on the lives of others; we bring peace and hope to troubled lives.

Seventeen

DIVINE OPTIMISM

Pessimism is antagonistic to the divine Idea. God is an eternal optimist; infinitely successful in all His undertakings. He has no thoughts of failure or despair or doubt. God can never be anything other than an optimist, for He *knows* that *all is well*. In the same way, if we think with God we naturally come in harmony with His Will and Purpose. We enter into the divine consciousness knowing that all is well. If we can see that although on the surface things may appear to be a mess, yet all is well with God's beautiful universe, we can never be a pessimist.

A pessimist is one who sees only the dark side of things and not knowing that these are the transient shadows, and that above is the eternal and perfect reality, becomes

plunged into despondency. The more he medi-
tates upon evil the more he believes in it. The
more he believes in it the more it grows.

Pessimism is a philosophy of despair.
It undermines the health; it holds one back
from success; it robs the life of all joy and
brightness, it makes one a depressing influence upon others. A pessimist is an enemy
to himself and a source of depression and
discord to others.

If the divine object of life is to come
into harmonious union with God, then all
pessimism must be replaced by an optimis-
tic attitude towards life, and by a confident
habit of thinking. No one who is a pessimist can know God, neither can one who
knows God be a pessimist. One who knows
God cannot help being an optimist, for he
knows that *all is well.*

A philosophy of truth induces optimism. It is founded on the firm belief that
the Creator knows what He is doing with
His universe and that, in an interior sense,

all is good and *all is well*. It believes that ultimately there is no power but God's power and that this is good. It asserts that man has only to come into harmony with the infinite Love and automatically, by the operation of changeless and infinitely just law, he will enter into peace, happiness, abundance and health; he will receive every good and perfect gift, not in some future time or place, but *here* and *now*.

Eighteen

THE GREATEST OF THESE IS
LOVE – St Paul

Love is the key to every situation in life; and by love is meant that kindly feeling that desires only the good for those we love. To cultivate thoughts of love, goodwill, forgiveness, pity, compassion, not only blesses and help others, but it also brings happiness and harmony into our own life. In the Sermon on the Mount we are told to agree with our adversary, and to love our enemies, and to do good to those who ill treat us. This commandment need not be a tedious restriction, but it is an open door through which we can pass into a richer and fuller life. If we follow this commandment or advice, our life becomes filled with blessing, and our difficulties are overcome in a wonderful way. If, when we meet difficult people we train ourselves to think thoughts of goodwill about them, and want positive things for them, we find that the difficulty is overcome, and harmony reigns instead. If certain people annoy us, and we allow ourselves to be annoyed, and if we sit in judgement upon them and magnify their faults and failings, then the annoyance increases, so that not only is our own life spoilt but also we make life more difficult for the one whom we think is the cause of the trouble. But if, instead of allowing ourselves to be annoyed, we envelop the people who 'rub us up the wrong way,' with thoughts of goodwill and try to look at things from their point of view, appreciating difficulties and troubles, and trying to see the God within them endeavouring to find expression then the whole situation becomes healed, and we are no longer annoyed. Also, through so doing we help the one who would otherwise annoy us, and this, of course, is the greatest thing we can do in life; help and bless other people, and enable them to unfold and reveal the hidden splendour.

Again, if the barking of a dog irritates us, then if we actively start loving the dog, and become sympathetic and compassionate, the barking will either stop or will no longer have the power to annoy us.

Yet, again, if street musicians or beggars annoy us, if we think lovingly of them, instead of resentfully, then they too cease to irritate us. Whatever the situation may be, and no matter how difficult, *love is the key*. Love, when applied in this way, heals every situation, smoothes every difficulty, and brings about a divine adjustment. When Jesus said that we should love one another, He gave us the secret of how to make our life harmonious, beautiful and happy. Many people have tried to follow the teaching of Jesus, simply as a commandment. They have tried to follow it because they have felt they ought to try to follow it, as a duty, if they are to be good Christians, but they have never realised, perhaps, that the advice of Jesus is not a boring and meaningless commandment, but an *open sesame* to a life of joy, freedom, and grace that is indescribable. If they had known this, they might have been more successful; for it is always easier to do a thing when we know the meaning of it, and what it is for, and what it leads to.

Then, again, many of those who have tried to follow the teaching have found it very difficult because they have not realised or understood the power of thought, or the necessity for training the thoughts to think in right channels. They have said: "But how can I love my enemies? I don't like them and never shall like them, so how can I feel love towards them?" However, I must point out that it is not a case of liking our enemies; and also, it is not a matter of feelings of affection. Love of the kind meant, is goodwill, compassion, tolerance and gentleness, giving of oneself, and one's very best to others. "God so loved the world that He gave His only begotten Son," is more understandable if we say: "God so pitied the world," or "God had such compassion for the world."

What I want to speak of in closing is how thought and thought control can be used by us to help us to love our enemies. Our natural feeling is to resent what our enemies do to us, and to think thoughts of antagonism, of self-justification and condemnation. Doing this increases the trouble and causes matters to go from bad to worse. Instead we can say: "I will not think thoughts of resentment or condemnation at all, but only thoughts of goodwill, forgiveness and compassion, and I will also pray that you may be blessed in every possible way." Then we can express our thoughts in definite words, such as: "So and so (mentioning the name of our enemy), I love you, I forgive you, even as God loves and forgives me. I pray that you may be blessed in every possible way, and that you may find God and be filled with unspeakable joy." When we start doing this we may feel very far from loving, but the spoken word, which is a formed thought, has power, and if we *persevere* day after day, we gradually become changed, until we really can love our enemy, and pray for his welfare as earnestly as for that of our nearest and dearest. When this is accomplished the whole situation is found to be healed.

Other titles by the Author

MY SEARCH FOR TRUTH   ISBN 0-9531597-7-9
THE STORY OF MY LIFE   ISBN 0-9531597-8-7
WITHIN YOU IS THE POWER   ISBN 0-9531597-2-8
THE POWER OF THOUGHT
LIFE WITHOUT STRAIN   ISBN 0-9531597-9-5
DIVINE ADJUSTMENT   ISBN 0-9531597-6-0
THE OPEN DOOR   ISBN 0-9531597-3-6
LIFE OF THE SPIRIT   ISBN-0-9531597-4-4
THE HAMBLIN BOOK OF DAILY READINGS
                              ISBN 0-9531597-5-2

Also recommended:

The River That Knows The Way
Edited by Stephanie Sorréll
ISBN 0-9531597-0-1

The Inner Temple by Hanne Jahr
ISBN 0-9531597-1-X

New Vision – a bi-monthly magazine
(formerly *Science of Thought Review*)
founded by Henry Thomas Hamblin

For further information contact the publisher:
Science of Thought Press Ltd.
Bosham House, Bosham, Chichester,
West Sussex PO18 8PJ, England

Telephone/Fax: +44 (0)1243 572109
E-mail: scienceofthought@mistral.co.uk

p 36 - 38.
p 43. - 45
p 45 - 47